GREAT MOMENTS IN AMERICAN HISTORY

"The British Are Coming!"

The Midnight Ride of Paul Revere

Nancy Golden

ROSEN CENTRAL
PRIMARY SOURCE™

THE ROSEN PUBLISHING GROUP, INC., NEW YORK

Published in 2004 by The Rosen Publishing Group, Inc.
29 East 21st Street, New York, NY 10010

Editor: Eric Fein
Book Design: Christopher Logan
Photo researcher: Rebecca Anguin-Cohen
Series photo researcher: Jeff Wendt

Photo Credits: Cover (left), title page, pp. 6, 10, 14, 22, 30, 32 © North Wind Picture Archives; cover
(right) illustration © Debra Wainwright/The Rosen Publishing Group; p. 18 © Burstein
Collection/Corbis; p. 29 Boston Athenaeum; p. 31 Courtesy of The Massachusetts Historical Society

First Edition

Publisher Cataloging Data

Golden, Nancy
    "The British are coming!" : the midnight ride of Paul Revere /
Nancy Golden.
    p. cm. — (Great moments in American history)
    Summary: Paul Revere, a member of the Sons of Liberty, travels on horseback to warn
the militia that the British regulars are coming by sea to destroy the colonists' weapons.
    ISBN 0-8239-4378-X (lib. bdg.)
    1. Revere, Paul, 1735-1818—Juvenile literature 2. Statesmen—Massachusetts—
biography—Juvenile literature 3. Massachusetts—Biography—Juvenile literature 4.
Massachusetts—History—Revolution, 1775-1783—Juvenile literature   [1. Revere,
Paul, 1735-1818   2. Statesmen 3. Massachusetts—History—Revolution, 1775-1783
4. United States—History—Revolution, 1775-1783]   I. Title II. Series 2004

973.3'311'092—dc21
[B]   2003-006787

Manufactured in the United States of America

CONTENTS

Preface

The American Revolutionary War was fought from 1775 to 1783. The war was between England and its American colonies. For many years before the war started, England had been placing high taxes on the goods the colonists bought from England. The colonists asked England to stop taxing them. England refused. This angered the colonists. The colonists refused to pay the taxes and they stopped buying goods made in England. British soldiers in the colonies tried to make the colonists follow England's laws. Soon, fighting between the colonists and the British soldiers broke out.

In Boston, Massachusetts, many colonists were against British rule. Paul Revere was one of these people. Paul Revere was a silversmith working in Boston. As a silversmith, Revere made many different items, such as bowls and cups, using silver.

Revere was a member of a group called the Sons of Liberty. The Sons of Liberty wanted to be free from British rule. The group had members in different towns in some of the thirteen colonies. In late November 1773, Revere began to work as a messenger for the Sons of Liberty. He carried important messages from town to town on horseback.

In the spring of 1775, British general Thomas Gage discovered that the colonists were storing weapons in Concord, a town near Boston. He also learned that two of the leaders of the Sons of Liberty, John Hancock and Samuel Adams were staying in Lexington. Lexington was another town near Boston. Gage began making plans to attack both towns.

Dr. Joseph Warren, an important leader of the colonists, discovered Gage's plans. He knew Gage had to be stopped. People in Lexington and Concord needed to be warned of the attack. Paul Revere would need to ride again . . . .

The Old North Church was built in the early 1700s. At the time, it was the tallest building in Boston.

Chapter One

THE EVENING BEGINS

I t is Tuesday, April 18, in the year 1775. My family and I have finished our evening meal. There is a knock on the door. My wife, Rachel, answers it.

"Dr. Warren needs to see Mr. Revere," I hear a voice say. "Right away!"

I grab my coat, kiss Rachel gently, and rush out of the house. Dr. Warren is one of the finest men I know. For many years, I have worked side by side with him in a group called the Sons of Liberty. We have been fighting against England for the rights of our people.

When we arrive at Dr. Warren's house, he opens the door himself. "Come in, Paul," he says. He leads me to a seat in front of the fireplace.

"It seems that General Gage is aware of your trips to Lexington. You've become quite famous for your rides." He laughs gently. "Tonight I am asking you to ride again. This may well be the most important journey you've ever made. We've received word that Gage has ordered his regulars to march on Concord." The regulars are what we call England's trained soldiers.

"Once there, they intend to destroy our supply of weapons," continues Dr. Warren. "They might even do harm to John Hancock and Samuel Adams who are in Lexington."

Hancock and Adams are very important leaders in our struggle for freedom. John Hancock is one of the area's richest businessmen. He is also one of our finest patriots. Samuel Adams is a member of the Massachusetts government.

"We must warn everyone of the British plans," I say.

"I have already sent out another messenger to go to Lexington," Dr. Warren says. "William

Dawes is his name. He is not as swift a rider as you are. However, he is less well known. Hopefully, he may be able to slip by the British without being noticed. Dawes has taken the route by land to Lexington. You shall go to Lexington by crossing the Charles River. Your first stop will be Boston's Charlestown section."

"Our people must know quickly if the regulars will be coming by land or by water," I say. "If we learn that the regulars are coming by land, we can hang one lantern from the top of the North Church here in Boston. If they are coming by sea, we can hang two lanterns. That will be our signal."

"A fine idea," Dr. Warren says. "Go safely."

I return to my house to say good-bye to Rachel.

"You will be careful, won't you?" she asks.

"I always am," I answer. "Keep safe inside."

I jump on my horse and ride off. I know I have a long evening ahead of me.

Paul Revere's midnight ride captured peoples' imaginations. Many artists drew or painted what they thought Revere's ride looked like. The poet Henry Wadsworth Longfellow even wrote a poem in 1860 called "Paul Revere's Ride."

Chapter Two

THE RIDE BEGINS

I ride like the wind to the north part of town where I keep a boat. At the river's edge, I see several of my friends standing by the landing. They have prepared my small boat.

"Hurry, Paul," they say. "We must leave quickly."

The British warship *Somerset* lies before us on the Charles River. We silently row our way across the river. The moon is bright in the night sky, but luck is on our side. We are not spotted by the British. Slowly, we move ahead. It is about eleven o'clock in the evening when we reach the shore of Charleston. Several of our patriot friends are waiting for us.

"We saw the signal in the church steeple," they say. "Two lanterns! The regulars are coming by sea."

My friends back in Boston had done their job well. When they learned how the British were coming, they went to the North Church and hung two lanterns.

"Yes," I say. "Now, we've got to warn Hancock and Adams!"

"We've already sent a messenger to Lexington," says Richard Devens. Devens is one of our finest patriot leaders. "I don't know if they've arrived though," he continues. "There are at least nine British soldiers guarding that road. They have fine horses and plenty of firearms!"

"Have you an equally fine horse for me?" I ask Devens.

"Our best," he says. "Brown Beauty. There's no faster horse in the county!"

"I hope you are right," I say, "for I will need both luck and speed tonight!"

"It is getting close to midnight," Devens says. "You must go."

"Farewell!" I say. "You are true friends."

"Friends and patriots together!" he shouts.

We wave good-bye, as I gallop off down the road.

The night is cool and clear as I ride. All is going well until I turn a corner and see two British officers on horseback. I am close enough to see that they have guns ready to be used.

I've been spotted! One of them rides toward me. The other seems to ride ahead. Perhaps his plan is to cut me off. I turn my horse off to the side and begin to gallop away. The soldiers turn and chase me, but my horse is too fast. Within moments, Brown Beauty and I leave the soldiers far behind. We continue on toward Lexington.

John Hancock (1737-1793) was an important American Revolutionary War leader. He was also the leader of the colonies' Continental Congress from 1775 to 1777.

Chapter Three

THE MEETING IN LEXINGTON

*I*t is midnight when I arrive in Lexington's town square. Lexington is about 11 miles northwest of Boston. I make my way to the home of Reverend Jonas Clarke. I have been here many times recently, visiting with Mr. Hancock and Mr. Adams.

The house is guarded by a sergeant and other members of the Lexington militia. Though the militia is made up of colonists, I do not know any of them. I call out to them as I approach.

"Who are you?" the sergeant asks.

"I don't have time to answer questions," I say loudly. "I must speak to the men inside!"

"Quiet down! The family has gone to bed!" he says.

"You'll have more than enough noise before long!" I yell. "The regulars are coming!"

I push past him and bang on the door with all my might. At the same time, the door opens and someone shouts, "Come in, Revere!"

Hancock and Adams are waiting for me inside.

"The regulars are on their way!" I say as I enter. "The two of you need to get out of Lexington!"

"Sit down," Adams says. "Tell us what you know."

I cannot sit. I pace back and forth in front of the fire, telling them what has happened. Within moments, the door opens again and in walks William Dawes. Dawes is the other messenger.

"I see you've all assembled without me," he says. "What is our plan?"

"Sit down, William, and I will tell you," I say. "We've got to get to Concord. We need to protect our weapon supplies. And our friends here *must* get moving. I fear they may be a target as well."

"Yes," Hancock says. "You might be right."

"Then we're off!" I say, and walk out the door.

Dawes is right behind me. We get on our horses and head for Concord. Concord is about 6 miles away.

As we ride, we meet another friend, Samuel Prescott. Prescott is a doctor in Concord and another member of the Sons of Liberty.

"Where are you off to in such a hurry?" Prescott asks.

We tell him about the British troops and about our plans. "I'd be honored to join you," says Prescott.

"And we'd be honored to have you," I say.

Soon, we come to a farmhouse. Prescott and Dawes slow down to see if anyone is at home. At that moment, I come face-to-face with two British soldiers. "Stop!" they say to me. "If you go an inch further, you are a dead man!"

"The famous Mr. Revere!" the officer exclaims. He calls out to the others. "Look who we have here!"

"Who is it, Major Mitchell?" they ask.

"Why it is the great messenger of the patriots, Paul Revere!"

"Ah, Mr. Revere," he says. "Where have you been riding tonight? Are you traveling across the land, telling stories to your friends?"

"Yes, I am, sir," I answer, with a bit of a smile. "All of my friends."

At that, the major grabs the reins of my horse from me. "Major Mitchell," I say. "Let me have my reins. I will not run from you."

"If you are Paul Revere," he says, "then I will not trust you. Your adventures are well known to all of us. Your time as messenger has come to an end. And if you attempt to run, we will be forced to kill you."

"You may do as you please," I reply.

We begin our ride back toward Lexington. As we get closer, we hear shots ring out.

"What was that?" one of the soldiers asks.

"Those were warning shots," I say calmly. "They are meant to let the townspeople know that your regulars are coming near."

Major Mitchell seems upset by my comment.

"What if there is trouble?" another soldier asks.

"We have no troops to back us up!" says another, worried. "We would surely lose a battle!"

"We will continue on," says Major Mitchell.

In a short time, more shots ring out. At this, all the soldiers become quite alarmed. I must say, the major looks quite alarmed himself!

"We must go and join our other troops," I hear Mitchell say. "They will be needing us."

"But what about Revere?" an officer asks.

"We'll free him," says Mitchell. "But we shall take his horse. Let the great Paul Revere continue his journey using feet, not hooves!"

They pull me from my horse. They ride off into the night, taking Brown Beauty with them.

With or without a horse, I must complete my mission. I cannot fail.

This picture shows the minutemen in battle with British soldiers at Lexington. Lexington is considered the place where the first battle in the American Revolutionary War was fought.

Chapter Five

THE BATTLE OF LEXINGTON

*I*t is past two o'clock in the morning as I make my way toward the center of Lexington. Arriving once again at Reverend Clarke's home, I am surprised to find Adams and Hancock still there. "Why haven't you left?" I ask. "You are in danger here!"

After much talking, the two of them agree to leave. They ride away in Hancock's carriage. Over the next hour, a steady flow of messengers arrives at the house. The messengers bring news of the British troops. Major John Pitcairn of the British Royal Marines has ordered six companies, or groups of soldiers, to begin marching to Concord. They could possibly arrive in Lexington soon.

There is another knock on the door. It is John Lowell, Hancock's young helper.

"Has something happened?" I ask. "Are Adams and Hancock alright?"

"They are fine, sir," he answers. "But Mr. Hancock has left something quite valuable behind."

"What is it?" I ask.

"A large trunk, filled with many important papers. It is at Buckman Tavern. Mr. Hancock fears that it might fall into the hands of our enemies. Can you help me move it to a safe place?"

I agree to help Lowell. Together we leave the house. By 4:30 that morning, Lowell and I arrive at Buckman Tavern. Men are gathered everywhere, sharing news.

"Pitcairn's companies will be here shortly," one says.

Lowell and I climb the stairs to the tavern's second floor. There we find the trunk. Looking out a window, we see John Parker, captain of the Lexington militia. He has gathered sixty or seventy of his men in Lexington Common. The minutemen, as they call themselves, are ready to fight. Looking in the opposite direction, we see Pitcairn's troops in the distance.

"We must get this trunk to a safe location before the British troops arrive!" I say to Lowell. We carry the heavy trunk down the narrow stairs, and out the front entrance of the tavern. Continuing across Lexington Common, we pass Captain Parker's men.

As we head for cover in an area of trees, I hear Parker's command to his troops. "Stand your ground! Don't fire unless fired upon!" he says. "But if they want to have a war, let it begin here!"

At this point, a large group of Pitcairn's soldiers move straight toward the Lexington militia. We can see several British officers on horseback, leading the other soldiers. They all have their muskets loaded and ready to fire.

"Move away!" one of the officers yells.

"Lay down your weapons!" another orders.

Captain Parker remains calm. "Spread out," he tells the militia, "and do not fire." There is a lot of disorder and noise. However, most of his men have heard his command. In the next second, though, we hear a shot. We can see a patch of smoke in front of

Pitcairn's soldiers. Did they fire the shot, or was it fired at them? We cannot tell.

What follows is the sound of more and more gunfire. When the smoke clears, we can see that several of our militiamen lay dead. Others are clearly hurt. Pitcairn's men move tensely, awaiting orders.

"On to Concord!" we hear Pitcairn cry. The soldiers fire their muskets in the air as a sign of victory, and then ride off.

"What will happen now?" Lowell says.

"I do not know," I say.

I would later find out that our forces in Concord fought bravely against the British soldiers. Though the British managed to destroy many of our weapons stored in Concord, they could not find them all. The British were outnumbered. They quickly headed for the safety of Boston. Though we lost many good men, we did not lose our desire for freedom. I believe believe that history will show that on this day we took the first steps on the road to freedom. And by making my midnight ride, I helped lead the way.

GLOSSARY

bridle (BRYE-duhl) the straps that fit around a horse's head and mouth and are used to control it

colonies (KOL-uh-neez) a territory that has been settled by people from another country and is controlled by that country

militia (muh-LISH-uh) a group of citizens who are trained to fight but who only serve in a time of emergency

patriot (PAY-tree-uht) someone who loves his or her country and is prepared to fight for it

reins (RAYNZ) straps attached to a bridle to control or guide a horse

sergeant (SAR-juhnt) an officer in the armed forces who is appointed from among the enlisted personnel

silversmith (SIL-vur-smith) someone who makes or repairs silver objects

steeple (STEE-puhl) a high tower on a church or other building

tavern (TAV-urn) a place where people can sit and drink alcoholic beverages

weapon (WEP-uhn) something that can be used in a fight to attack or defend, such as a sword, gun, knife, or bomb

Primary Sources

*H*ow can we learn about the people, places, and events of long ago? One way is to study sources such as old letters, maps, photos, and drawings. These sources let us understand history as it was happening. For example, the map on page 29 shows Boston as it looked in 1775. By studying the map, we can compare and contrast how that city looked then to how it looks today. Without sources such as this map, we would have no idea how Boston looked over two hundred years ago.

The list from one of Revere's record books, shown on page 31, allows us to determine the kinds of items Revere made and for whom he made them. For example, we can see that he made silver buckles for the shoes of a man named Joshua Brackett. Studying original sources, such as Revere's business records, helps us understand what life was like as a silversmith.

This map of Boston was done in 1777. It shows where the British soldiers were based in 1775. The map was based on information from many people, including a British soldier, Lieutenant Page.

Samuel Adams (1722-1803) was an important leader in Boston. He was a member of the Continental Congress. He was also governor of Massachusetts from 1794 to 1797.

This is a page from one of Paul Revere's record books from his silversmith business. This page is from January 8, 1763. It is a list of his customers and what he made for them.

This picture shows the colonists fighting British soldiers at Concord. The Battle of Concord started at the Old North Bridge, which was over the Concord River.